W9-AVL-401

CONTENTS

Tara Lipinski

PRACTICE MAKES PERFECT

Do you dream of being a top skater? Would you wake up at three in the morning to practice? Tara Lipinski did.

U.S.A.

Olympic Champion, 1998

World Champion, 1997

BIRTHDAY: June 10, 1982

HOBBIES: sewing, collecting frogs

**WEB SITE:
www.taralipinski.com**

A few years after Tara began skating, she moved to Texas. There were few rinks and little ice time in Texas. The only time Tara could practice was in the middle of the night. So, for two years, that is what she did. Every day, by the time school started, Tara had already practiced on the ice for almost three hours.

When Tara jumps, she turns quickly and tightly in the air.

Tara loved skating, but those early practices made her so tired. Tara's mom and dad decided that something had to change. So Tara and her mom moved to Delaware and then to Michigan, where she could get more ice time. Finally Tara could train during the day.

Tara missed her dad, but she loved skating. She was very talented and learned quickly. By the time Tara was 14, she was the world's best skater. One year later, she was Olympic Champion. All those early-morning practices paid off.

Elvis Stojko

FOCUS ON A DREAM

Everyone thought Elvis Stojko would win the 1998 Olympics. He was the World Champion, and he had won the silver medal at the last Olympics.

But Elvis had a secret. He was badly injured and in great pain. Only his family and coaches knew. He didn't want people to feel sorry for him. He didn't want to talk about the pain. Elvis wanted to focus on his skating.

Elvis loves performing and the crowds love him.

CANADA

Olympic Silver, 1994, 1998

World Champion, 1994, 1995, 1997

BIRTHDAY: March 22, 1972

HOBBIES: dirt-bike racing, martial arts

4

Practices were torture for Elvis. He still kept his secret. Other athletes would have dropped out of the Olympics, but not Elvis. When it came time to perform, Elvis spun and jumped like a champion.

As soon as Elvis finished skating, his face twisted in pain. Finally the whole world knew his secret. Elvis limped to the boards. His coach had to help him off the ice. But Elvis had skated his best. Despite being so badly injured, he won a silver medal.

Jenni Meno and Todd Sand

LOVE MAKES IT HAPPEN

Jenni Meno and Todd Sand began skating together because of love. They were skating with different partners. Then Jenni and Todd fell in love. They decided to become a skating team.

Jenni and Todd's love made it easier for them to practice long hours. Soon they became the best American pairs team.

Jenni and Todd love skating and love each other.

U.S.A.
U.S. Champions, 1994–96
BIRTHDAYS:
November 11, 1970 (Jenni)
October 30, 1963 (Todd)

FAVORITE FOODS:
anything Mexican (Jenni)
chocolate chip ice cream
(Todd)

6

These skaters are always perfectly in step. Jenni and Todd move as gracefully as ballet dancers. That makes their skating look romantic.

After being the top U.S. pair for three years in a row, Jenni and Todd were injured. They could not skate their best. Other teams beat them. But Jenni and Todd still had each other.

At the 1998 Olympics, Jenni and Todd skated badly. They were very disappointed. But they knew that the World Championships were only one month away. Jenni and Todd wanted to skate their best there. And they did. They won silver, their highest result ever.

Irina Slutskaia

TAKING THE WORLD BY STORM

Most kids start figure skating for fun. Not Irina Slutskaia. She started skating because she was always sick. Irina's mom wanted Irina to skate outside in the fresh air. She thought it would help clear up Irina's terrible colds.

Irina hated skating at first. She cried and would not let go of her mom's hand. But it was not long before Irina wanted to skate by herself. The exercise was fun. Irina's colds got better.

RUSSIA
European Champion, 1995
BIRTHDAY: February 9, 1979
HOBBY: collecting stuffed animals

Irina is the first Russian woman to become European Champion.

Irina now practices six days a week. The Typhoon wins skating contests all over the world. But she remembers who helped her get started. With the prize money from one of her first competitions, Irina bought her parents a new car.

Soon Irina had lots of energy. Her grandmother nicknamed her "the Typhoon." (A typhoon is a huge storm, bigger than a hurricane.) Irina still jumps and speeds around the ice like a typhoon. You would never know that she was once so sick.

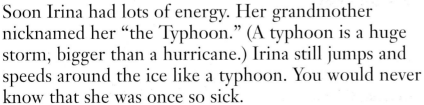

Elizabeth Punsalan and Jerod Swallow

COURAGE TO CHANGE

Did you know that ice dancers practice their routines for months? It takes that long to learn them perfectly. Once the competition season starts, the routines almost never change.

U.S.A.

U.S. Champions, 1991, 1994, 1996–98

BIRTHDAYS:
September 1, 1971 (Liz)
October 18, 1966 (Jerod)

HOBBIES:
gardening (Liz)
collecting art (Jerod)

Elizabeth Punsalan and Jerod Swallow carefully prepared their routines for the 1998 Olympics. It was their last season to compete. They wanted it to be their best. Liz and Jerod were skating well. They won their first contest of the season.

Then everything went wrong. After one bad result, Liz and Jerod's coach said that the judges didn't like one of their routines. So Liz and Jerod did the impossible. They changed the routine only weeks before the Olympics.

The team started from scratch. Liz and Jerod even chose new music. Months of work were crammed into weeks. Sometimes they practiced all night.

Liz and Jerod have perfect timing and perfect positions.

Liz and Jerod had little time to make their routine perfect. But that is what they did. Their hard work paid off. At the Olympics, Liz and Jerod skated without a mistake.

Todd Eldredge

COMMUNITY SPIRIT

Most skaters depend on their families for help. Parents drive them to practices and pay the bills. Brothers and sisters cheer from the stands. Todd Eldredge's family and his entire hometown of Chatham, Massachusetts, helped him.

As Todd's skating improved, he needed more ice time and coaching. Todd's parents couldn't pay for it all. So the people of Chatham started to raise money for Todd.

Todd became a fast and smooth skater. He jumped high and far. When he became one of the world's best skaters, his town was very proud.

U.S.A.
World Champion, 1996
BIRTHDAY: August 28, 1971
HOBBY: golf

12

Todd can spin fast and in many different positions.

Then Todd was injured. Skating became a struggle. Finally Todd quit. But he realized that even when he had skated poorly, his town cheered for him. Todd returned to the ice. He was ready to soar again.

Todd was thrilled to become World Champion in 1996. His prize money helped pay back his parents. Todd also presented a check to his hometown. Winning was the best way to thank his parents and his town.

Elena Berezhnaia and Anton Sikharulidze

DARE TO TRY AGAIN

S katers have many struggles. Sometimes it is hard to get ice time. Paying the coach can be tough, too. But one of a skater's biggest problems is beating serious injuries.

RUSSIA
Olympic Silver, 1998
World Champions, 1998, 1999

BIRTHDAYS:
October 20, 1977 (Elena)
October 25, 1976 (Anton)

HOBBIES:
painting (Elena)
football, cars (Anton)

This pair is strong, as well as graceful and smooth.

Once more, Elena dared to try. She and Anton Sikharulidze, her new partner, competed after skating together only nine months. They were very nervous.

In less than two years, Elena and Anton became World Champions. Elena's courage put them on top.

Elena Berezhnaia knows about injuries. One day she and her pairs partner spun too close to each other. Suddenly his skate blade split open her head. Elena was rushed to the hospital. The blade had cut so deep it had damaged her brain. People wondered if Elena would walk again.

Elena was used to overcoming problems. After all, she was a skater. So Elena taught herself to walk. Just three months after the accident, she even skated. But would Elena risk performing again?

Ilia Kulik

THE WILL TO WIN

Ilia is known for his huge jumps but he also has interesting positions.

Can you imagine wanting something badly enough to leave your country and your family? That's what Ilia Kulik did. He left Russia and moved to the United States. He wanted to train with a coach who could help him win Olympic gold.

His new coach was great. But Ilia missed his family. To make things worse, he had trouble skating his best. Ilia was out of shape. He knew he had to work harder.

Ilia trained for months to make his jumps look powerful and easy. But top skaters need more than great jumps. So Ilia's coach helped him add smoothness and grace to his skating.

RUSSIA
Olympic Champion, 1998
BIRTHDAY: May 23, 1977
HOBBIES: boxing, shooting

16

Finally Ilia's moment came: the 1998 Olympics. This was why he had given up so much. Ilia skated his best performance ever. The judges thought so, too.

What did Ilia do when he finished performing? He called his mom to share his gold-medal news.

Shae-Lynn Bourne and Victor Kraatz

GO FOR IT

Watch Shae-Lynn Bourne and Victor Kraatz skate. Do you feel like joining them on the ice? Shae-Lynn and Victor want you to feel as if you are dancing with them. This team loves skating for a crowd.

Shae-Lynn and Victor are champs because they look like each other's shadow when they skate.

CANADA

Canadian Champions, 1993–99

BIRTHDAYS:
January 24, 1976 (Shae-Lynn)
April 7, 1971 (Victor)

FAVORITE FOODS:
angel hair pasta (Shae-Lynn)
lobster (Victor)

Shae-Lynn and Victor don't look like many of the other ice dancers. Most teams are dramatic and serious. Shae-Lynn and Victor are full of fun and energy. They are fast skaters, and their feet move quickly.

At the 1998 Olympics, Shae-Lynn and Victor received more applause than any other dance team. They did not win a medal, but Shae-Lynn and Victor won over the audience. That's what really counts for this team.

Amazing moves are what Shae-Lynn and Victor are known for. Hydroblading is one of their favorites. They each balance on one skate blade, then lean toward the ice. Their bodies glide over the ice, almost touching it. Shae-Lynn and Victor say that hydroblading makes them feel as if they are floating.

Michael Weiss

BE YOURSELF

When Michael Weiss started to skate, his parents could not afford to buy him new skates. So they took an old pair of his sister's white skates and painted them black.

U.S.A.
U.S. Champion, 1999
BIRTHDAY: August 2, 1976
HOBBIES: hockey, golf

Other kids made fun of Michael when the black paint chipped off. White spots showed up all over his skates. It took guts for him to ignore them. Michael fought back the best way he could — he just kept skating.

20

No one makes fun of Michael now. In fact, he likes being different. He skates in a T-shirt to rock music while others dress up and perform to classical music.

Michael is also one of the first figure skaters to lift weights. Weight lifting gives Michael power and confidence. That helps him take risks.

Every day Michael skates for four hours and lifts weights.

In 1998 Michael had to fight for a place on the U.S. Olympic team. He became the first skater to attempt the most difficult quadruple jump. It was not perfect, but he had the courage to try. Because of his gutsy effort, he made the team.

Anjelika Krylova and Oleg Ovsiannikov

READY FOR THE TOP

Figure skaters must always be prepared. A skate lace can come undone at the last minute. Or a costume can rip just before a contest.

Anjelika Krylova and Oleg Ovsiannikov know what being ready means. They often placed second in national competitions. But they felt ready to be first.

Anjelika and Oleg are known for their smoothness and grace.

RUSSIA
Olympic Silver, 1998
World Champions, 1998, 1999
BIRTHDAYS:
July 4, 1973 (Anjelika)
January 23, 1970 (Oleg)
HOBBIES:
disco-dancing (Anjelika)
video games (Oleg)

But Anjelika and Oleg raced to the competition. They got there just in time to practice. This team was ready to perform. They skated beautifully and won the top prize. Anjelika and Oleg were finally ready for first place.

This ice dance team knew its turn would come. So Anjelika and Oleg practiced and improved quickly. Their chance came when they did not expect it.

Another Russian dance team dropped out of a contest at the last minute. Anjelika and Oleg were asked to compete. There was no time to prepare. Many teams would have said no.

Tanja Szewczenko

STARTING OVER

Tanja Szewczenko was only one year old when she first saw people skating. She wanted to skate, too. So her grandmother surprised her with new skates on her second birthday. Tanja was so happy she cried!

Skating became Tanja's favorite thing to do. She was very good at it. But when she was 18, Tanja became so sick she could not skate. She was really weak. Even getting out of bed was impossible. Tanja's illness was serious. Would she ever skate again?

GERMANY

German Champion, 1994, 1995

BIRTHDAY: July 26, 1977

HOBBIES: reading, writing to pen pals

Tanja is known for her fast skating and tight spins.

The medical help that Tanja needed cost a lot. Her parents spent almost all their money to make their daughter healthy. Tanja slowly began to feel better. She amazed her doctors. Tanja even started to skate again.

Tanja entered her first competition just months later. She placed first! Skating again made Tanja feel great. Giving her prize money to her parents felt even better.

Oksana Kazakova and Artur Dmitriev

BATTLING TO BE BEST

Most skaters love taking their bows after a performance. They are glad it is over. Not Artur Dmitriev. He loves to compete, and he hates losing.

RUSSIA
Olympic Champions, 1998

BIRTHDAYS:
April 8, 1975 (Oksana)
January 21, 1968 (Artur)

HOBBIES:
pool (Oksana)
tennis, skiing (Artur)

Artur and his pairs partner, Oksana Kazakova, do whatever it takes to skate their best. They practice for hours to improve their jumps, lifts and throws. Oksana and Artur know that when they skate well, they win.

It is difficult to always skate perfectly. Sometimes Oksana and Artur make mistakes. But this team learns from its errors.

Oksana and Artur are fast and exciting skaters.

Artur was so happy when he and Oksana made the 1998 Olympic team. Finally they would compete in the biggest contest of all. That didn't make Oksana and Artur nervous. It made them try harder. They earned the top prize: the gold medal.

Oksana and Artur talk with their coach when things go wrong. Then they spend hours fixing the problems. After one bad season, Artur decided to train harder and lose weight. Oksana learned to control her nerves.

Alexei Yagudin

THE POWER OF A DREAM

When Alexei Yagudin was 11, he had a special dream. He wanted to buy his family a home of its own.

RUSSIA
World Champion, 1998, 1999
BIRTHDAY: March 18, 1980
HOBBIES: fishing, watching movies

Alexei grew up sharing an apartment with another family. That's how many Russian families live. Alexei hated it. He wanted his own home. But how could an 11-year-old boy earn that much money?

It was clear that Alexei was a good skater. So he decided to become a prize-winning skater. That way, Alexei could earn money and make his dream come true.

Alexei can perform quadruple jumps. Most skaters can only do triples.

Alexei began to work hard. He had nerves of steel and amazing jumps. Jumps are the most important part of men's skating. In 1997 Alexei won the bronze medal at the World Championships. He was only 16. That win took him a step closer to his dream.

Just one year later, Alexei won the gold medal at Worlds. With the prize money from his win, Alexei's dream could come true. He could finally buy his family a home.

Michelle Kwan
GRACE AND COURAGE

When Michelle was 13 years old, she became the youngest American to compete at the World Championships.

Does Michelle Kwan remind you of a ballet dancer when she skates? She moves so smoothly and gracefully.

U.S.A.
Olympic Silver, 1998
World Champion, 1996, 1998
BIRTHDAY: July 7, 1980
HOBBY: fishing
FAVORITE FOOD: Belgian waffles

Michelle was seven when she first saw skaters compete at the Olympics. She decided that she wanted to go to the Olympics, too. Michelle did not know how much practice that would take. She soon learned.

The tough training did not bother Michelle. She loved to learn new skills. Michelle became known for her great jumps and fabulous spins. By the time she was 15, Michelle was World Champion.

Michelle's performances amazed the crowds. Then she began to feel nervous in competition. The whole world watched her struggle. Michelle never gave up. Instead, she practiced even more. Soon she had climbed back to the top.

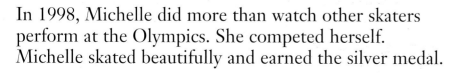

In 1998, Michelle did more than watch other skaters perform at the Olympics. She competed herself. Michelle skated beautifully and earned the silver medal.

For Wendy, Mary Lynn, Rick and Maurice — blood is thicker than water

Acknowledgments

Many thanks to the following people who helped me with this book:
Lisa Carey, Irene Stojko, Audrey Weisiger, Lorna Wighton and Tracy Wilson.

Thanks also to Kids Can's publishers, Valerie Hussey and Ricky Englander,
for their faith in me; Liz MacLeod, the most supportive editor in the world;
and designer Julia Naimska, whose creativity makes this book stand out.

My gratitude also extends to my kids, Ashleigh, Robert and Michael,
who are extremely encouraging. And the last thanks is reserved for
my husband, Bob, my biggest fan of all.

Photo credits

Marc Evon, Wintersport Products & Images: cover (top left, center), 2, 3 (left), 11 (left),
19 (left), 29 (both). **©Ice Castle:** 31 (left). **Stephan Potopnyk:** 5 (right), 10, 15 (left), 16, 19 (right),
21 (right), 26, 27 (left), 30. **Cam Silverson:** cover (bottom left, top and bottom right), 3 (right),
4, 6, 7 (both), 8, 9 (both), 11 (right), 12, 13 (both), 14, 15 (right), 17 (both), 18, 21 (left),
22, 23 (both), 24, 25 (both), 27 (right), 28, 31 (right), back cover (both).
Irene Stojko Collection: 5 (left). **Audrey Weisiger Collection:** 20.

Printed in Hong Kong by Sheck Wah Tong Printing Press Limited.

Canadian Cataloguing in Publication Data

Cranston, Patty
The best on ice : The world's top figure skaters
ISBN 1-55074-581-6

1. Skaters – Juvenile literature. 2. Skating – Juvenile literature. I. Title.
GV850.A2C727   1999   j796.91'20922   C99-930359-7

Kids Can Press is a Nelvana company